Ramadan and Id-ul-Fitr

Nancy Dickmann

Heinemann Library
Chicago, Illinois

www.heinemannraintree.com

Visit our website to find out more information about Heinemann-Raintree books.

To order:

☎ Phone 888-454-2279

🖥 Visit www.heinemannraintree.com to browse our catalog and order online.

Edited by Sian Smith, Nancy Dickmann, and Rebecca Rissman
Designed by Steve Mead
Picture research by Elizabeth Alexander
Production by Victoria Fitzgerald
Originated by Capstone Global Library Ltd
Printed and bound in China by South China Printing Company Ltd

The content consultant was Richard Aubrey. Richard is a teacher of Religious Education with a particular interest in Philosophy for Children.

14 13 12 11 10
10 9 8 7 6 5 4 3 2 1

Library of Congress Cataloging-in-Publication Data
Dickmann, Nancy.
  Ramadan and Id-ul-Fitr / Nancy Dickmann.
    p. cm.—(Holidays and Festivals)
  Includes bibliographical references and index.
  ISBN 978-1-4329-4049-2 (hc)—ISBN 978-1-4329-4068-3 (pb)
1. Ramadan. 2. 'Id al-Fitr. 3. Fasts and feasts—Islam. I. Title.
  BP186.4.D55 2011
  297.3'62—dc22   2009054305

Acknowledgments
We would like to thank the following for permission to reproduce photographs: Alamy pp. **5** (© Louise Batalla Duran), **8** (© T. Kopecny), **10** (© Art Directors & TRIP), **11**, **23 top** (© imagebroker), **15** (© David Noble Photography), **19** (© Sally and Richard Greenhill); Corbis pp. **4**, **23 bottom** (© epa), **20** (© Arshad Arbab/epa); Getty Images pp. **13** (Gen Nishino/Taxi), **14** (Chumsak Kanoknan), **16** (Marco Di Lauro/The Image Bank), **18** (arabianEye); Photolibrary pp. **7** (Paul Thuysbaert/GraphEast), **21** (Corbis); Shutterstock pp. **6** (© Distinctive Images), **9** (© Dennis Albert Richardson), **12** (© Kate Fredriksen), **22 left** (© gpalmer), **22 right** (© Faraways), **23 middle** (© Serp); World Religions Photo Library p. **17**.

Front cover photograph of Muslims celebrating the end of Ramadan, Colombo, Sri Lanka reproduced with permission of Photolibrary (Dominic Sansoni/Imagestate RM). Back cover photograph reproduced with permission of Alamy (© Art Directors & TRIP).

We would like to thank Diana Bentley, Dee Reid, Nancy Harris, and Richard Aubrey for their invaluable help in the preparation of this book.

Every effort has been made to contact copyright holders of any material reproduced in this book. Any omissions will be rectified in subsequent printings if notice is given to the publisher.

Contents

What Is a Festival?

A festival is a time when people come together to celebrate.

4

Muslim people celebrate Ramadan and Id-ul-Fitr.

Ramadan

Ramadan is the holiest month for Muslim people.

It is a time to feel close to Allah,
or God.

People pray during Ramadan.

They pray in a mosque.

People may eat before the Sun comes up.

People should not eat or drink during the day. This is called fasting.

People may eat again when the Sun goes down.

Ramadan lasts for a month.

Id-ul-Fitr

At the end of Ramadan, Muslim people celebrate Id-ul-Fitr.

new moon

People wait until they see the
new moon.

mosque

People then go to the mosque
to pray.

People can stop fasting. They can eat
at any time.

People visit friends and family.

They share a special meal.

They give food to the poor.

They share snacks, candy, and gifts.

Look and See

new moon

candy

Have you seen these things?
They make people think of Ramadan
and Id-ul-Fitr.

Picture Glossary

 **fasting** to go without food and water

 **mosque** building where Muslims go to worship

 **Muslim people** people who follow the teachings of the religion Islam

Index

Note to Parents and Teachers

Before reading

Ask the children to think of as many holidays and festivals as they can. Look at the list together and discuss which holidays and festivals are religious. Explain that Ramadan and Id-ul-Fitr are festivals celebrated by Muslim people, who follow the religion of Islam. Ramadan is a holy time for Muslims because the verses of the Qur'an (the Muslim holy book) were revealed to the prophet Muhammad during this month. Reading the Qur'an is an important part of Ramadan. The festival of Id-ul-Fitr comes after Ramadan and means the 'festival of breaking of the fast.'

After reading

• Explain that remembering the poor is another important part of Ramadan, and that fasting (explained on page 11) can be a way for people to remind themselves of what it is like to be poor. Ask the children if they can think of ways to help the poor in the local area.

• Ask the children if there are things that they would find it hard to go without. Encourage them to choose something (such as computer games or snacks) to give up for a day or a week. Afterward, discuss what it was like to go without something they wanted. Explain that during Id-ul-Fitr, Muslims thank Allah for the help and strength that he gave them throughout Ramadan to help them practice self-control.